Spelling Practice Book 4

By Janey Pursglove
with additional material by Jenny Roberts
Series developed by Ruth Miskin
Spelling consultant: Jennifer Chew

Contents

OXFORD

Adding the prefix mis- and revising un-, in-, dis-

Speed spell

Write the **Speed spell** words.

a _____ b _____ c _____

d _____ e _____ f _____

Circle any errors. Write the corrected spellings in your Log Book.

Spelling zone (online)

1 Read and then complete the statement below with your partner.

A _____ is a group of letters we can add to the **front** of a root word to change its meaning.

2 Add the prefix **mis-** to these words to give their opposite meaning.

mis lead   _____ behave

_____ understand   _____ place

3 Write the correct word from the box above to match each definition.

a _____ to put something in the wrong location

b _____ to deliberately give someone the wrong idea

4 Now add the correct prefix **un-, in-, dis-** or **mis-** to these words to give their opposite meaning.

_____ correct   _____ appear   _____ happy

_____ fair   _____ match   _____ complete

Dots and dashes

Dot and dash the graphemes in the words.
Write the number of sounds.

misbehave	**8**	misprint		misunderstand	
misplace		disagree		mismatch	
mislead		unfair		undo	
misspell		mistreat		inhuman	

 The word **misspelt** is often misspelt! It keeps the **s** from **mis** and the **s** from **spelt**.
mi**s** + **s**pelt   mi**ss**pelt

Word changers

Complete the table.

prefix	root word	prefix + root word
mis-		misbehave
in-	active	
un-		unfair
mis-	match	
mis-		mistrust
in-	human	
un-		unkind
mis-	spell	
mis-		misunderstand
dis-	agree	

Words to log and learn

Choose five words from **Dots and dashes** and **Word changers**
that you find hard to spell. Write them on p.22 of your Log Book.
Circle the part of the word that you find the hardest to remember.
Explain to your partner why and discuss how you will learn it.

Dictation

Take turns to read aloud one of the dictation sentences from Unit 1, p.62
(Partner 1) and p.63 (Partner 2) for your partner to write down. After each
sentence, correct any errors, then swap.

1 _____

_____

2 _____

_____

Four-in-a-row

Choose a word from **Dots and dashes** or **Word changers** and say
it to your partner. Ask them to write it down.
Circle any wrong letters. If the word is right, tick a shape in your partner's
book. Can you both spell four in a row correctly?

◯ ◯ ◯ ◯   ◯ ◯ ◯ ◯   ◯ ◯ ◯ ◯

_____

_____

Choose the right word

Complete the sentences using the correct word from each word family.

> trust   mistrust   mistrusted   spell   misspell
> misbehave   behave   lead   mislead

1   The Prince was right to _____ the naughty elf.

2   Do you _____ me to look after your hamster?

3   Try not to _____ the head teacher's name.

4   Is it possible to learn how to _____
    all the words in this dictionary?

5   Max trained his dog to _____ ,
    so that it always did what Max told it to.

6   Most children probably _____ at some time
    when they are little.

7   Do not _____ me by pretending you know all
    the answers!

8   I have a map, so I shall _____ you all back to the camp.

Team teach

Now work together to play **Team teach**.

Jumping orange words

Write the words you have been revising with your teacher below.

_____   _____   _____

_____   _____

Words ending in *zhuh* spelt -sure

Speed spell

Write the **Speed spell** words.

a _____ b _____ c _____

d _____ e _____ f _____

Circle any errors. Write the corrected spellings in your Log Book.

Spelling zone

1 Read the rule with your partner.

> The ending that sounds like **zhuh** can be spelt **-sure** at the end of a word.

2 Take turns to say the words. Exaggerate the **-sure** ending.

mea**sure**   trea**sure**   plea**sure**   enclo**sure**   lei**sure**

3 Write the correct word from the box above to match each definition.

a _____ the feeling you have when you take enjoyment from something

b _____ to find out the size of something

c _____ something precious and valuable

d _____ free time to use as you please

e _____ something surrounded by a boundary

4 Circle each of the three syllables in the word **enclosure**.

Dots and dashes

Dot and dash the graphemes in the words. Write the number of sounds.

treasure	5	enclosure	
measure		pleasure	
leisure		closure	

 Notice that in the word **leisure** the *e* sound is spelt **ei**.

Revision

picture	5	mixture	
adventure		creature	
capture		puncture	

Word changers

Complete the table.

Tip: Remember to drop the final **e** from the root word if a suffix begins with a vowel.

root word	suffix	root word + suffix
pleasure	-s	
treasure	-ed	
measure	-ment	
measure	-ing	
leisure	-ly	
capture	-ing	
picture	-ed	

Words to log and learn

Choose five words from **Dots and dashes** and **Word changers** that you find hard to spell. Write them on p.23 of your Log Book. Circle the part of the word that you find the hardest to remember. Explain to your partner why and discuss how you will learn it.

Dictation

Take turns to read aloud one of the dictation sentences from Unit 2, p.62 (Partner 1) and p.63 (Partner 2) for your partner to write down. After each sentence, correct any errors, then swap.

1 _____

_____

2 _____

_____

Four-in-a-row

Choose a word from **Dots and dashes** or **Word changers** and say it to your partner. Ask them to write it down. Circle any wrong letters. If the word is right, tick a shape in your partner's book. Can you both spell four in a row correctly?

☆ ☆ ☆ ☆   ☆ ☆ ☆ ☆   ☆ ☆ ☆ ☆

_____

_____

Choose the right word

Complete the sentences using the correct word from each word family.

> leisurely   leisure   pleasure   pleasures
> measurement   measure   measuring
> treasured   treasures   treasuring

1   I am going to take a _____ walk.

2   In my _____ time, I like to ride my bike.

3   The leaflet listed the _____ of Cornwall.

4   Mum said it was a _____ to spend time with Gran.

5   I was _____ my height when the tape broke.

6   How can you _____ the size of the Earth?

7   We took a precise _____ of the length
    of the beetle.

8   This lovely picture is my most _____ possession.

9   We found some amazing _____ in the
    box in the attic.

Team teach

Now work together to play **Team teach**.

Jumping orange words

Write the words you have been revising with your teacher below.

_____   _____   _____

_____   _____   _____

Special focus 1

The short *u* sound spelt ou

1 Read the information with your partner.

> Sometimes the letters **ou** in a word make the short vowel sound *u*.
>
> I love d**ou**ble scoop ice creams!

2 With a partner, read the words and underline where the letters **ou** make the *u* sound. The first one has been done for you.

> tr**ou**ble   enough   toughest
>
> rougher   young   country

3 Complete each sentence using the correct word from the box below.

> double   touch   trouble   youngest
>
> younger   country   enough

a Our teacher said we must not _____ anything on the wall.

b Your apple is _____ the size of mine.

c Eva is _____ than me.

d Josh is the _____ of the children in his family.

e There is not _____ cheese on my pizza.

f I knew we'd be in _____ with Dad for walking inside with muddy boots on.

g Every _____ in the world has its own flag.

Adding the prefix **auto-**

Speed spell

Write the **Speed spell** words.

a _____ b _____ c _____

d _____ e _____ f _____

Circle any errors. Write the corrected spellings in your Log Book.

Spelling zone (online)

1 Read the rule with your partner.

> The prefix **auto-** means 'self' or 'own'. We can just add it to the front of words without changing their spelling.

2 Add the prefix **auto-** and then take turns to read the words.

auto graph _____ pilot _____ matic

3 Write the correct word from the box below to match each definition.

> **auto**mobile   **auto**biography   **auto**cue

a _____ a book telling the story of the writer's own life

b _____ a device that shows a script for a speaker or performer

4 Write a sentence using any word with the prefix **auto-**.

_____

Dots and dashes

Dot and dash the graphemes in the words. Write the number of sounds.

automobile	8	autopilot	
autograph		autobiography	
autocue		automatic	

 The word **mobile** rhymes with **smile** but the word **auto**mobile rhymes with **feel**. Very weird!

Word changers

Complete the table.

Tip: The plural of **autobiography** is **autobiographies**. We change the **y** to an **i** before adding **-es**.

prefix	root word	prefix + root word	+ suffix -s or -es
auto-	pilot	autopilot	autopilots
		automobile	
auto-	biography		
		autocue	
auto-	graph		

Words to log and learn

Choose five words from **Dots and dashes** and **Word changers**
that you find hard to spell. Write them on p.24 of your Log Book.
Circle the part of the word that you find the hardest to remember.
Explain to your partner why and discuss how you will learn it.

Dictation

Take turns to read aloud one of the dictation sentences from Unit 3, p.62
(Partner 1) and p.63 (Partner 2) for your partner to write down. After each
sentence, correct any errors, then swap.

1 _____

_____

2 _____

_____

Four-in-a-row

Choose a word from **Dots and dashes** or **Word changers** and say
it to your partner. Ask them to write it down.
Circle any wrong letters. If the word is right, tick a shape in your partner's
book. Can you both spell four in a row correctly?

△ △ △ △   △ △ △ △   △ △ △ △

_____

_____

Choose the right word

Complete the sentences using the correct word.

> biography   autobiography   autobiographies   autopilot
> pilot   autocue   cue   automatic   automobile   mobile

1 When I am older, I will write my _____ .

2 I would like to read a _____ of the first
man on the moon.

3 I believe that my grandfather was
a _____ .

4 Most new aeroplanes have an
_____ system.

5 The actor waited at the side of
the stage for his _____ .

6 The newsreader looked at the
_____ for what to say next.

7 The doors are _____ so you
don't have to push them open.

8 This American _____ needs lots of fuel.

Team teach

Now work together to play **Team teach**.

Jumping orange words

Write the words you have been revising with your teacher below.

_____   _____   _____

_____   _____   _____

Adding the suffix -ly

Speed spell

Write the **Speed spell** words.

a _____   b _____   c _____

d _____   e _____   f _____

Circle any errors. Write the corrected spellings in your Log Book.

Spelling zone

1 Read the information and the
   words with your partner.

> We can add the suffix **-ly** to an adjective to
> make an adverb: breezy   breez**ily**

2 Which letter is swapped for an **i** before the suffix **-ly** is added?

> We swap _____ for an **i** before adding the suffix _____ .

3 Take turns to read these adverbs.

> happ**ily**   angr**ily**   merr**ily**   cheek**ily**   sleep**ily**

4 Change the adverbs back into adjectives.

> _____ happy   _____   _____
>
> _____   _____

> **Tip:**   If a word ends with **ic**, add the suffix **-ally** not **-ly**:
>
> fran**tic** fran**tically**   drama**tic** drama**tically**
>
> Say **cally** to rhyme with **Sally** to help you to spell these words.

Dots and dashes

Dot and dash the graphemes in the words.
Write the number of sounds.

angry	5	frantic		automatic	
sleepy		magic		nice	
sad		comic		cosy	
hasty		dramatic		slow	
happy		physical		final	

Word changers

Complete the table.

> **Tip:** Remember to check whether you need to change the **y** to an **i** before you add **-ly**.

adjective	suffix	adverb
cheeky	-ly	cheekily
rude	-ly	
angry	-ly	
sad	-ly	
heavy	-ly	
bossy	-ly	
heroic	-ally	heroically
magic	-ally	
automatic	-ally	
comic	-ally	

Words to log and learn

Choose five words from **Dots and dashes** and **Word changers** that you find hard to spell. Write them on p.25 of your Log Book. Circle the part of the word that you find the hardest to remember. Explain to your partner why and discuss how you will learn it.

Dictation

Take turns to read aloud one of the dictation sentences from Unit 4, p.62 (Partner 1) and p.63 (Partner 2) for your partner to write down. After each sentence, correct any errors, then swap.

1 _____

_____

2 _____

_____

Four-in-a-row

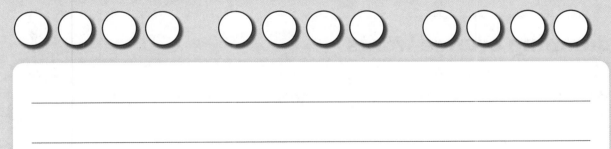

Choose a word from **Dots and dashes** or **Word changers** and say it to your partner. Ask them to write it down. Circle any wrong letters. If the word is right, tick a shape in your partner's book. Can you both spell four in a row correctly?

◯ ◯ ◯ ◯   ◯ ◯ ◯ ◯   ◯ ◯ ◯ ◯

_____

_____

Choose the right word

Complete the sentences using the correct word.

> sadly   sad   angrily   angry   anger
> sleep   sleepily   haste   hastily   hasty

1 Nita felt _____ when her rabbit died.

2 Back at home, they unpacked their suitcases _____, knowing the holiday was over.

3 I was really _____ when I thought that someone had stolen my game.

4 The famous film star answered the rude question _____, then slammed the door.

5 Dad yawned _____ as he said, "It's been a long day!"

6 Beauty pricked her finger and fell into a deep _____.

7 Gran said a _____ goodbye, then rushed off to her exercise class.

8 I ate my dinner _____ because I didn't want to miss the start of the film.

Team teach

Now work together to play **Team teach**.

Jumping orange words

Write the words you have been revising with your teacher below.

_____   _____   _____

_____   _____   _____

Adding the prefix **inter-**

Speed spell

Write the **Speed spell** words.

a _____ b _____ c _____

d _____ e _____ f _____

Circle any errors. Write the corrected spellings in your Log Book.

Spelling zone (online)

1 Read the information with your partner.

> The prefix **inter-** means 'among' or 'between'. We can just add it to the front of words without changing their spelling.

2 Add the prefix **inter-** to these words. Take turns to read them.

Inter net _____ galactic _____ national _____ act

> **Tip:** The word **Internet** is spelt with a capital **I**.

3 Write the correct word to match each definition.

a _____ between different nations

b _____ between galaxies

c _____ a network of computers that communicate with one another

d _____ to have an effect on someone or something else

Dots and dashes

Dot and dash the graphemes in the words. Write the number of sounds.

intergalactic	12	international	
Internet		interrelate	
interact		intercity	
interlock		intermediate	

Word changers

Complete the tables.

prefix	root word	prefix + root word
inter-	city	intercity
inter-	national	
inter-	relate	
inter-	act	

Revision

prefix	root word	prefix + root word
		subway
super-	market	
		antifreeze
		submarine

Dictionary challenge

With your partner, find the words **meddle** and **medal** in a dictionary. Read the definitions aloud. Which one (**meddle** or **medal**) might you win in an international gymnastics competition?

Words to log and learn

Choose five words from **Dots and dashes** and **Word changers**
that you find hard to spell. Write them on p.26 of your Log Book.
Circle the part of the word that you find the hardest to remember.
Explain to your partner why and discuss how you will learn it.

Dictation

Take turns to read aloud one of the dictation sentences from Unit 5, p.62
(Partner 1) and p.63 (Partner 2) for your partner to write down. After each
sentence, correct any errors, then swap.

1 _____

_____

2 _____

_____

Four-in-a-row

Choose a word from **Dots and dashes** or **Word changers**
and say it to your partner. Ask them to write it down.
Circle any wrong letters. If the word is right, tick a shape
in your partner's book. Can you both spell four in a row correctly?

_____

_____

Choose the right word

Complete the sentences using the correct word from each word family.

> international   national   intercity   city
> interact   interactive   Internet   intermediate

1   Can you describe your country's _____ flag?

2   Each country sent their leader to an _____ meeting.

3   Edinburgh is the capital _____ of Scotland.

4   The fastest _____ trains can travel at more than 300 kilometres per hour.

5   The touch-screen exhibit at the museum was _____.

6   In a play, characters _____ with one another to tell a story.

7   When you learn to swim, you start in the beginner class, then move up to the _____ class. Finally, you can go to the advanced class.

8   I like finding information on the _____.

Team teach

Now work together to play **Team teach**.

Jumping orange words

Write the words you have been revising with your teacher below.

_____   _____   _____

_____   _____   _____

Special focus 2

Homophones

1 Read the information with your partner.

> Words that sound the same but have different meanings and spellings are called **homophones**.
> The Greek word for *same* is **homo**.
> The Greek word for *sound* is **phone**.
> **homophone** = *same sound*
> pair   pear

2 Take turns to read these sets of homophones.

> groan grown   main mane   reign rain rein
>
> peace piece   berry bury

3 Write the correct word from the box above to match each definition.

a _____ a sound someone might make when disappointed or in pain

b _____ the long hair on an animal's neck

c _____ the period of time that a King or Queen rules over a country

d _____ a slice or bit of something

e _____ what a pirate might do with treasure

f _____ one of the two long straps used to guide a horse

g _____ a type of fruit

h _____ wet weather

Words with the *ay* sound spelt **eigh, ei, ey**

Speed spell

Write the **Speed spell** words.

a _____ b _____ c _____

d _____ e _____ f _____

Circle any errors. Write the corrected spellings in your Log Book.

Spelling zone

1 Read the information with your partner.

> Sometimes the *ay* sound is spelt **eigh, ei** or **ey**.

2 Take turns to read the sound box and the words.

ay	
eigh	eight neighbour sleigh weigh
ei	vein veil reign
ey	obey they grey prey

3 Underline the part of each word in the box above that spells the *ay* sound.

 The word **reign** has a silent **g**.
The *ay* sound is spelt **ei**.

4 Find the homophones for these words in the box above.

ate _____   slay _____

pray _____   way _____

Dots and dashes

Dot and dash the graphemes in the words.
Write the number of sounds.

grey	3
eight	
vein	
veil	
obey	

prey	
neigh	
eighty	
weigh	
they	

rein	
sleigh	
weight	
freight	
eighteen	

Vocabulary check

The word **freight** means goods carried by road, rail, air or sea.

Word changers

Complete the table.

root word	suffix	root word + suffix
weight	-less	weightless
obey	-ed	
		reigned
		weighed
prey	-ed	
sleigh	-s	
		veins
		neighbours
grey	-ness	
		weighing
neighbour	-ly	

25

Words to log and learn

Choose five words from **Dots and dashes** and **Word changers** that you find hard to spell. Write them on p.27 of your Log Book. Circle the part of the word that you find the hardest to remember. Explain to your partner why and discuss how you will learn it.

Dictation

Take turns to read aloud one of the dictation sentences from Unit 6, p.62 (Partner 1) and p.63 (Partner 2) for your partner to write down. After each sentence, correct any errors, then swap.

1 _____

_____

2 _____

_____

Four-in-a-row

Choose a word from **Dots and dashes** or **Word changers** and say it to your partner. Ask them to write it down. Circle any wrong letters. If the word is right, tick a shape in your partner's book. Can you both spell four in a row correctly?

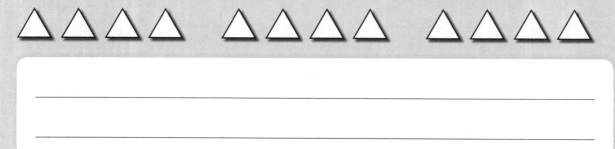

△ △ △ △   △ △ △ △   △ △ △ △

_____

_____

Choose the right word

Complete the sentences using the correct word.

> weight   weightless   reigned   reign   rein
>
> disobey   obey   eight   ate

1 Feathers are so light they feel almost _____ .

2 At the airport, we had to check the _____ of our luggage.

3 The Prince looked forward to the day when he would _____ over the nation.

4 Queen Victoria _____ for more than 60 years.

5 I took the _____ and led the new pony around the field.

6 Most children _____ their teacher.

7 If you _____ the rules, you may be punished.

8 I am inviting _____ children to my birthday party.

Team teach

Now work together to play **Team teach**.

Jumping orange words

Write the words you have been revising with your teacher below.

_____   _____   _____

_____   _____   _____

Words ending in -ous

Speed spell

Write the **Speed spell** words.

a _____   b _____   c _____

d _____   e _____   f _____

Circle any errors. Write the corrected spellings in your Log Book.

Spelling zone

1 Take turns to read the information and the words.

> The suffix **-ous** can just be added to some root words. When we say it aloud, it sounds like *us*.
>
> mountain   mountain**ous**   danger   danger**ous**
>
> In these words, we keep the **e** so that the **g** is a **soft g**.
>
> courage   courage**ous**   outrage   outrage**ous**

> If a root word ends in **our**, we have to **swap** the letters **our** for **or** before adding the suffix -**ous**.
>
> hum~~our~~   hum**or** + **ous**   hum**orous**

 Weird Word Warning! The *us* sound spelt **ous** is already part of these root words:

seri**ous**   curi**ous**   hide**ous**   anxi**ous**   obvi**ous**

2 Circle the word above that has an **e** before **ous** instead of an **i**.

3 Complete the sentence using the correct word from the box below.

> courageous   humorous   curious   glamorous

> I was _____ to know what was inside the cave.

Dots and dashes

Dot and dash the graphemes in the words. Write the number of sounds.

s·e·r·i·ou·s	6	tremendous	
obvious		jealous	
hideous		enormous	
anxious		glamorous	

Word changers

Complete the tables.

> **Tip:** Remember to check whether you need to make any changes to the root word before adding the suffix.

root word	root word + suffix -ous
courage	courageous
outrage	
poison	
humour	
mountain	
glamour	

root word	root word + suffix -ly
serious	
	hideously
obvious	
	jealously
	curiously
anxious	

Words to log and learn

Choose five words from **Dots and dashes** and **Word changers**
that you find hard to spell. Write them on p.28 of your Log Book.
Circle the part of the word that you find the hardest to remember.
Explain to your partner why and discuss how you will learn it.

Dictation

Take turns to read aloud one of the dictation sentences from Unit 7, p.62
(Partner 1) and p.63 (Partner 2) for your partner to write down. After each
sentence, correct any errors, then swap.

1 _____

_____

2 _____

_____

Four-in-a-row

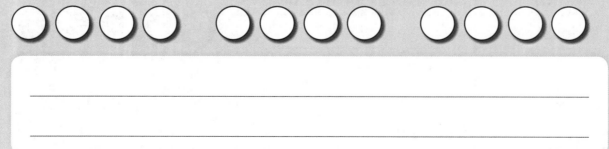

Choose a word from **Dots and dashes** or **Word changers**
and say it to your partner. Ask them to write it down.
Circle any wrong letters. If the word is right, tick a shape
in your partner's book. Can you both spell four in a row correctly?

◯ ◯ ◯ ◯   ◯ ◯ ◯ ◯   ◯ ◯ ◯ ◯

_____

_____

Choose the right word

Complete the sentences using the correct word from each word family.

> curiously   curious   obvious   obviously
>
> courageous   courage   courageously   humorous   humour

1   I am _____ about the birthday surprise.

2   They peered _____ through the crack in the wall.

3   This _____ belongs to you – it has your name on it.

4   The room was silent – it was _____ that no one knew the answer.

5   The firefighter showed great _____ when she rescued the child.

6   Molly was very _____ when she told the teacher about the bullies.

7   Mr Witts has a great sense of _____ and always makes us laugh.

8   My uncle is famous for his _____ jokes.

Team teach

Now work together to play **Team teach**.

Jumping orange words

Write the words you have been revising with your teacher below.

_____   _____   _____

_____   _____   _____

Words with the **s** sound spelt **sc**

Speed spell

Write the **Speed spell** words.

a _____   b _____   c _____

d _____   e _____   f _____

Circle any errors. Write the corrected spellings in your Log Book.

Spelling zone

1 Read the information with your partner.

> Sometimes the **s** sound is spelt **sc**. It can occur at the beginning or the middle of a word.

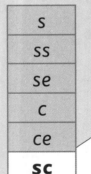

2 Take turns to read the sound box and the words.

s
ss
se
c
ce
sc

> **sc**ent   **sc**ience   **sc**ene   **sc**issors
>
> fa**sc**inate   mu**sc**le   a**sc**end   de**sc**end

3 Choose three words from the box above that you think are the most useful to know how to spell. Write them here.

_____   _____   _____

> **Tip:** Try sounding the **c** as **k** when spelling these words. It sounds very odd but will help you to remember to add the silent **c**.

Dots and dashes

Dot and dash the graphemes in the words.
Write the number of sounds.

sc i ss or s	5	ascend	
science		descend	
scent		muscle	
scene		fascinate	

Word changers

Complete the table.

> **Tip:** Remember to **drop** the **e** at the end of a root word before adding a suffix that starts with a vowel, such as -**ing** or -**ed**.

root word	suffix	root word + suffix
ascend	-ing	
ascend	-ed	
descend	-ed	
descend	-ing	
scene	-s	
scent	-s	
scent	-ed	
fascinate	-ing	
fascinate	-ed	
muscle	-s	

Words to log and learn

Choose five words from **Dots and dashes** and **Word changers**
that you find hard to spell. Write them on p.29 of your Log Book.
Circle the part of the word that you find the hardest to remember.
Explain to your partner why and discuss how you will learn it.

Dictation

Take turns to read aloud one of the dictation sentences from Unit 8, p.62
(Partner 1) and p.63 (Partner 2) for your partner to write down. After each
sentence, correct any errors, then swap.

1 _____

_____

2 _____

_____

Four-in-a-row

Choose a word from **Dots and dashes** or **Word changers**
and say it to your partner. Ask them to write it down.
Circle any wrong letters. If the word is right, tick a shape in
your partner's book. Can you both spell four in a row correctly?

_____

_____

Choose the right word

Complete the sentences using the correct word from each word family.

> muscle   muscles   scent   scented   unscented
> descend   descended   descending   scene   scenes
> fascinate   fascinated   fascinating

1 The champion had huge _____ in his arms!

2 I pulled a _____ in my leg during football.

3 A wonderful smell came from the _____ flowers.

4 The wolf picked up the _____ of its prey.

5 The spaceship was _____ from the night sky.

6 I knew I had to _____ the rickety old staircase.

7 The forest looked just like a _____ from a fairy tale.

8 My friend is in all three _____ of the school play.

9 It was _____ to watch the scientist at work.

10 I became _____ by the shapes
of the clouds.

Team teach

Now work together to play **Team teach**.

Jumping orange words

Write the words you have been revising with your teacher below.

_____	_____	_____
_____	_____	_____

Possessive apostrophes with plural words

1   Take turns to read the information.

> A possessive apostrophe shows that something belongs to someone or something else.
>
> > The boy**'s** dog. (The dog belongs to one boy.)
>
> If something belongs to more than one person or thing, the possessive apostrophe comes after the **s** of the plural word.
>
> > The boy**s'** dog. (The dog belongs to more than one boy.)

2   Put the apostrophe in the correct place in the plural words below. The first one has been done for you.

   a   Some of the boys' coats were left on the bus by mistake.

   b   All the teachers name badges were muddled up.

   c   The girls bikes were muddy after the ride through the woods.

3   Take turns to read the information.

> Remember that some plural words do not end in **s**.
>
> > children   men   women   geese   mice
>
> If we want to make these words possessives, we add '**s**.
>
> > The children'**s** books.

4   Put the apostrophe in the correct place in the plural words below.

   a   The womens changing rooms.

   b   The mens department.

Words ending in *zhun* spelt -sion

Speed spell

Write the **Speed spell** words.

a _____ b _____ c _____

d _____ e _____ f _____

Circle any errors. Write the corrected spellings in your Log Book.

Spelling zone

1 Take turns to read the words and the information.

> confuse   revise   explode   divide   decide

> When these words are changed into nouns, they end in *zhun* spelt **-sion**.

2 Exaggerate the ending as you read these nouns.

> confu**sion**   revi**sion**   explo**sion**
> divi**sion**   deci**sion**

3 Complete each sentence using the correct word from the box above.

a Even from far away, we could hear the _____ of the firework.

b We made the _____ to run for the bus.

c There was a lot of _____ in the changing room and I lost my shoes!

Dots and dashes

Dot and dash the graphemes in the words.
Write the number of sounds.

invade	5
explode	
divide	
collide	

confuse	
televise	
erode	
decide	

Vocabulary check

The word **erode** means 'wear away'. It is usually used to talk about cliffs and rocks worn away by the sea.

Word changers

Complete the table. (The noun is the verb with the **-sion** ending.)

Tip: Remember to **drop** the final **e** and the final consonant when adding **-sion** to make a noun.

verb	noun
televise	television
revise	
confuse	
invade	invasion
explode	
divide	
decide	
erode	

Words to log and learn

Choose five words from **Dots and dashes** and **Word changers** that you find hard to spell. Write them on p.30 of your Log Book. Circle the part of the word that you find the hardest to remember. Explain to your partner why and discuss how you will learn it.

Dictation

Take turns to read aloud one of the dictation sentences from Unit 9, p.62 (Partner 1) and p.63 (Partner 2) for your partner to write down. After each sentence, correct any errors, then swap.

1 _____

_____

2 _____

_____

Four-in-a-row

Choose a word from **Dots and dashes** or **Word changers** and say it to your partner. Ask them to write it down.
Circle any wrong letters. If the word is right, tick a shape in your partner's book. Can you both spell four in a row correctly?

△ △ △ △   △ △ △ △   △ △ △ △

_____

_____

Choose the right word

Complete the sentences using the correct word from each word family.

> invade   invasion   invaded   division   divide
> confuse   confusion   confuses   explosion   explode

1   What happened when the Romans _____ Britain?

2   The King announced that there would
    be an _____ of the country.

3   I am certain that my team will play
    in the top _____ this season.

4   Did you remember to _____ the
    pizza into four slices?

5   No one knew the words to the song or when
    to start, so it ended in _____!

6   Too much information can _____ people.

7   The film producers used special effects to create the
    _____ .

8   We watched the fireworks _____ in the night sky.

Team teach

Now work together to play **Team teach**.

Jumping orange words

Write the words you have been revising with your teacher below.

_____   _____   _____

_____   _____   _____

Adding il- and revising un-, in-, mis-, dis-

Speed spell

Write the **Speed spell** words.

a _____ b _____ c _____

d _____ e _____ f _____

Circle any errors. Write the corrected spellings in your Log Book.

Spelling zone

1 Read the information with your partner.

> Before root words beginning with **l**, the prefix **in-** becomes **il-**.
> It changes a word to give its opposite meaning.
> No changes are made to the root word before we add **il-**.

2 Add **il-** to the words below to create antonyms.

_**il**_ logical   _____ legal   _____ legible

3 Write the correct word to match each definition.

_____ against the law

_____ impossible to read

_____ without good reason

> **Tip:** Some other prefixes that change a word to give the opposite
> meaning are **un-**, **in-**, **mis-** and **dis-**.

Dots and dashes

Dot and dash the graphemes in the words.
Write the number of sounds.

legal	**5**	appear		complete	
agree		clear		literate	
polite		legible		kind	
logical		like		correct	

Word changers

Complete the table.

> **Tip:** Remember that **im-** goes before root words beginning with **m** or **p**.
> **im** + perfect   **im**perfect

prefix	root word	prefix + root word
il-	logical	illogical
un-		unkind
im-		impatient
dis-	qualify	
il-		illiterate
un-	clear	
il-		illegal
im-	practical	
il-		illegible
dis-	obey	

Words to log and learn

Choose five words from **Dots and dashes** and **Word changers** that you find hard to spell. Write them on p.31 of your Log Book. Circle the part of the word that you find the hardest to remember. Explain to your partner why and discuss how you will learn it.

Dictation

Take turns to read aloud one of the dictation sentences from Unit 10, p.62 (Partner 1) and p.63 (Partner 2) for your partner to write down. After each sentence, correct any errors, then swap.

1 _____

_____

2 _____

_____

Four-in-a-row

Choose a word from **Dots and dashes** or **Word changers** and say it to your partner. Ask them to write it down. Circle any wrong letters. If the word is right, tick a shape in your partner's book. Can you both spell four in a row correctly?

○ ○ ○ ○   ○ ○ ○ ○   ○ ○ ○ ○

_____

_____

Choose the right word

Complete the sentences using the correct word from each word family.

> literate illiterate impatient patient patients
> illegal legal practical impractical practically

1 In Victorian times, very few children went to school, so many people were _____ .

2 If you are _____ , you are able to read lots of different books.

3 I love celebrations so I am _____ for the next festival.

4 Thank you for being so _____ and waiting for me to arrive.

5 I believe it's _____ to smuggle pets onto aeroplanes.

6 Illegal is the opposite of _____ .

7 You have to be very _____ to work out how to put up the shelves.

8 It's _____ to try to carry everything at once.

Team teach

Now work together to play **Team teach**.

Jumping orange words

Write the words you have been revising with your teacher below.

_____   _____   _____

_____   _____   _____

Unit 11

The *c* sound spelt -**que** and the *g* sound spelt -**gue**

Speed spell

Write the **Speed spell** words.

a _____ b _____ c _____

d _____ e _____ f _____

Circle any errors. Write the corrected spellings in your Log Book.

Spelling zone

1 Take turns to read the information and the words.

> The ending -**que** sounds like **c** as in **c**at. It comes from the French spelling of the **c** sound.
>
> > che**que**   anti**que**   grotes**que**   uni**que**
>
> The ending -**gue** sounds like **g** as in **g**ate. It comes from the French spelling of the **g** sound.
>
> > catalo**gue**   lea**gue**   ton**gue**   dialo**gue**

2 Write the correct word from the box above to match each definition.

a _____ an old object

b _____ words spoken by characters

c _____ so special there is only one like it

d _____ something disgusting or repulsive, like a monster

e _____ a paper slip that is a form of payment

Dots and dashes

Dot and dash the graphemes in the words.
Write the number of sounds.

unique	4
cheque	
antique	

grotesque	
fatigue	
colleague	

catalogue	
dialogue	
league	

Word changers

Complete the table.

root words ending in -que	root word + suffix
	uniquely
	cheques
	grotesquely
	antiques
root words ending in -gue	**root word + suffix**
	fatigued
	cataloguing
	colleagues
	leagues

Words to log and learn

Choose five words from **Dots and dashes** and **Word changers**
that you find hard to spell. Write them on p.32 of your Log Book.
Circle the part of the word that you find the hardest to remember.
Explain to your partner why and discuss how you will learn it.

Dictation

Take turns to read aloud one of the dictation sentences from Unit 11, p.62
(Partner 1) and p.63 (Partner 2) for your partner to write down. After each
sentence, correct any errors, then swap.

1 _____

_____

2 _____

_____

Four-in-a-row

Choose a word from **Dots and dashes** or **Word changers** and say
it to your partner. Ask them to write it down.
Circle any wrong letters. If the word is right, tick a shape in your partner's
book. Can you both spell four in a row correctly?

☆☆☆☆ ☆☆☆☆ ☆☆☆☆

_____

_____

Choose the right word

Complete the sentences using the correct word from each word family.

> antiques   antique   cataloguing   catalogues   catalogue
> cheque   cheques   tongues   tongue

1 Jack took the old clock to the shop that
   sold _____.
2 My bike is so old it's almost an _____!
3 We can choose Asha a present by looking in
   these _____.
4 He saw the game he wanted in the _____.
5 The school trip and the lunch money had
   to be paid for with two separate _____.
6 I went to the bank with Mum to cash the only
   _____ I got for my birthday.
7 Our _____ were green after chewing the strange sweets.
8 It hurts when you bite your _____ by mistake.

Team teach

Now work together to play **Team teach**.

Jumping orange words

Write the words you have been revising with your teacher below.

_____   _____   _____

_____   _____   _____

Homophones

1 Tell your partner what a **homophone** is. Check your answer on p.23.

2 Take turns to read these pairs of homophones.

> heal   heel   missed   mist   who's   whose

3 Complete each sentence using the correct homophone from the box above.

a This blister on my heel will probably take ages to _____ .

b Mum almost _____ the turning to the farm because of the thick mist.

c We know whose bag it is but _____ going to return it to her?

4 Take turns to read the information and the words.

> Some words are 'near-homophones', e.g. quite/quiet. They sound similar but not exactly the same:
>
> accept   except   affect   effect

5 Complete each sentence using the correct near-homophone from the box above.

a The whole team went up to _____ the award, except Sam, who was poorly that day.

b I tried out a scary special effect on my brother but it didn't _____ him at all!

Adding **ir-** to words beginning with **r**

Speed spell

Write the **Speed spell** words.

a _____ b _____ c _____

d _____ e _____ f _____

Circle any errors. Write the corrected spellings in your Log Book.

Spelling zone

1 Take turns to read the words and the information.

> irregular   irresistible   irresponsible

> Before root words beginning with **r**, the prefix **in-** becomes **ir-**. It changes a word to give its opposite meaning.
>
> **ir**regular   **ir**resistible   **ir**responsible

2 Complete each sentence using the correct word from the box above.

a The party food was so delicious it was _____ .

b The buses arrived at quite _____ times.

c It was _____ to let that dog off its lead.

Revision

3 Read and complete the sentence below with your partner. (Check p.41 if you need a reminder.)

> Before root words beginning with **l**, the prefix **in-** becomes _____ .

Dots and dashes

Dot and dash the graphemes in the words.
Write the number of sounds.

relevant	8
practical	
correct	
resistible	

connect	
perfect	
tidy	
fair	

responsible	
logical	
appear	
patient	

Word changers

Complete the table.

prefix	root word	prefix + root word
ir-	relevant	irrelevant
ir-		irregular
ir-	resistible	
ir-	responsible	
un-		unfair
dis-	agree	
im-		impractical
il-	logical	
mis-		misspell

Dictionary challenge

With your partner, find the words **fair** and **fare** in a dictionary. Read the definitions aloud. Then add the correct words (**fair** or **fare**) below.

Her hair was very _____ .

I paid the train _____ .

Words to log and learn

Choose five words from **Dots and dashes** and **Word changers**
that you find hard to spell. Write them on p.33 of your Log Book.
Circle the part of the word that you find the hardest to remember.
Explain to your partner why and discuss how you will learn it.

Dictation

Take turns to read aloud one of the dictation sentences from Unit 12, p.62
(Partner 1) and p.63 (Partner 2) for your partner to write down. After each
sentence, correct any errors, then swap.

1 _____

_____

2 _____

_____

Four-in-a-row

Choose a word from **Dots and dashes** or **Word changers**
and say it to your partner. Ask them to write it down.
Circle any wrong letters. If the word is right, tick a shape
in your partner's book. Can you both spell four in a row correctly?

△ △ △ △   △ △ △ △   △ △ △ △

_____

_____

Choose the right word

Complete the sentences using the correct word from each word family.

> regular   irregular   regularly   irrelevant   relevant
> legible   illegible   irresponsible   responsible   responsibility

1 You should eat fruit _____ as part of a healthy diet.

2 The coloured beads were not in an exact order so they formed an _____ pattern.

3 That information is from last year, so it is _____ now.

4 This TV programme about the Tudors is _____ to the history topic that you are doing at school this term.

5 Matt's handwriting is much better. It is neat and _____.

6 The note pinned to the door was _____ because it got soaked in the rain.

7 Who is _____ for the mess in this classroom?

8 Walking on the frozen pond was extremely dangerous and _____.

Team teach

Now work together to play **Team teach**.

Jumping orange words

Write the words you have been revising with your teacher below.

_____   _____   _____

_____   _____   _____

Adding the suffix -ion (1)

Speed spell

Write the **Speed spell** words.

a _____ b _____ c _____

d _____ e _____ f _____

Circle any errors. Write the corrected spellings in your Log Book.

Spelling zone

1 Take turns to read the information and the words.

The sound **shun** at the ends of words can be spelt in different ways.

If the root word ends in **ss**, just add **-ion**.

confe**ss** + **-ion**   confe**ssion**

posse**ss** + **-ion**   posse**ssion**

2 Change the verb **express** into a noun ending in **-ion**.

express _____

 The letter **t** in the words **permit**, **submit** and **transmit** must be **swapped** for **ss** before we add **-ion**.

permi~~t~~   permi**ss** + **ion**   permi**ssion**

3 Change the verb **admit** into a noun ending in **-ion**.

admit _____

Dots and dashes

Dot and dash the graphemes in the words.
Write the number of sounds.

discuss	6
permit	
confess	
depress	

submit	
possess	
admit	
transmit	

progress	
impress	
process	
express	

Word changers

Complete the table.

> **Tip:** Remember to **swap** the **t** with **ss** before adding **-ion** if a word ends in **-mit**.

root word	root word + suffix -ion
possess	
express	
confess	
progress	
discuss	
impress	
admit	admission
permit	
transmit	
submit	

Words to log and learn

Choose five words from **Dots and dashes** and **Word changers**
that you find hard to spell. Write them on p.34 of your Log Book.
Circle the part of the word that you find the hardest to remember.
Explain to your partner why and discuss how you will learn it.

Dictation

Take turns to read aloud one of the dictation sentences from Unit 13, p.62
(Partner 1) and p.63 (Partner 2) for your partner to write down. After each
sentence, correct any errors, then swap.

1 _____

_____

2 _____

_____

Four-in-a-row

Choose a word from **Dots and dashes** or **Word changers**
and say it to your partner. Ask them to write it down.
Circle any wrong letters. If the word is right, tick a shape
in your partner's book. Can you both spell four in a row correctly?

◯ ◯ ◯ ◯   ◯ ◯ ◯ ◯   ◯ ◯ ◯ ◯

_____

_____

Choose the right word

Complete the sentences using the correct word from each word family.

admit   admission   discussed   discussion   discuss
progress   progressed   possess   possession

1   The _____ fee was too expensive for us.

2   I must _____ that it was me who broke it.

3   How long do you think the _____ between the politicians will last?

4   The girls sat in the library and _____ the problem until they had solved it.

5   The carnival _____ slowly down the street.

6   Has there been much _____ in my writing?

7   The burglar stole my favourite _____ .

8   "When we marry, we will share everything we _____ !" said the Prince.

Team teach

Now work together to play **Team teach**.

Jumping orange words

Write the words you have been revising with your teacher below.

_____   _____   _____

_____   _____   _____

Adding the suffix -ion (2)

Speed spell

Write the **Speed spell** words.

a _____   b _____   c _____

d _____   e _____   f _____

Circle any errors. Write the corrected spellings in your Log Book.

Spelling zone

1 Take turns to read the verbs ending in **d** and the information.

> exten**d**   comprehen**d**   expan**d**   suspen**d**

> We can add the suffix **-ion** to change these verbs into nouns.
> We must **swap** the **d** for an **s** before adding **-ion**.
>
> expan~~d~~   expan**s** + **ion**   expan**sion**

2 Change the verbs into nouns. The first one has been done for you.

expand   <u>expansion</u>   comprehend _____

extend _____   suspend _____

3 Take turns to read the words ending in **se** and the information.

> preci**se**   confu**se**   ten**se**   revi**se**

> We can add the suffix **-ion** to change these words into nouns.
> We must **drop** the **e** before adding **-ion**.
>
> precis~~e~~   precis + **ion**   preci**sion**

4 Change the words into nouns. The first one has been done for you.

precise _____precision_____ confuse _____

tense _____ revise _____

Dots and dashes

Dot and dash the graphemes in the words. Write the number of sounds.

tense	4	comprehend		pretend	
suspend		precise		expand	
extend		confuse		revise	

Word changers

Complete the table.

> **Tip:** Think carefully about which letters to **drop** or **swap** before adding the suffix **-ion**.

root word	root word + suffix -ion
confuse	confusion
tense	
precise	
revise	
expand	expansion
suspend	
extend	
comprehend	

Words to log and learn

Choose five words from **Dots and dashes** and **Word changers**
that you find hard to spell. Write them on p.35 of your Log Book.
Circle the part of the word that you find the hardest to remember.
Explain to your partner why and discuss how you will learn it.

Dictation

Take turns to read aloud one of the dictation sentences from Unit 14, p.62
(Partner 1) and p.63 (Partner 2) for your partner to write down. After each
sentence, correct any errors, then swap.

1 _____

_____

2 _____

_____

Four-in-a-row

Choose a word from **Dots and dashes** or **Word changers**
and say it to your partner. Ask them to write it down.
Circle any wrong letters. If the word is right, tick a shape
in your partner's book. Can you both spell four in a row correctly?

☆ ☆ ☆ ☆   ☆ ☆ ☆ ☆   ☆ ☆ ☆ ☆

_____

_____

Choose the right word

Complete the sentences using the correct word from each word family.

> tension   tense   tensed   confuse   confusion
> revision   revise   revised   expand   expansion   expanded

1 I was very _____ and nervous before I went on the stage.

2 After the argument, everyone felt the _____ in the room.

3 When the bouncy castle started to collapse,

   I lost my sock in all the _____ .

4 Please don't _____ me with too
   much information!

5 We must _____ for the test tomorrow.

6 Did you remember to do the _____ for the test?

7 These plans show the _____ of the school grounds.

8 The seating area in the hall had to be _____ to
   make space for the school concert.

Team teach

Now work together to play **Team teach**.

Jumping orange words

Write the words you have been revising with your teacher below.

_____   _____   _____

_____   _____   _____

Partner 1 dictation sentences

Unit 1

Do not misbehave in the library.
I must not misplace my kit.

Unit 2

We need to measure that circle.
Ross will build an enclosure.

Unit 3

I asked for her autograph.
TV presenters often use autocues.

Unit 4

The unicorn magically appeared.
Sam slammed the door grumpily.

Unit 5

I learnt about the Internet today.
It was fun watching the kittens interact.

Unit 6

Remember to obey the safety rules.
We did eight exercises in PE.

Unit 7

What you said was outrageous.
She was very jealous of Snow White.

Unit 8

My muscles hurt after that exercise.
The plane will descend soon to land.

Unit 9

It was a big explosion.
I can imagine his confusion.

Unit 10

My great-grandfather was illiterate.
The man gave an illogical answer.

Unit 11

My antique chair is unique.
May I look at the games catalogue?

Unit 12

It is irresponsible to swim here.
We have tea at irregular times at home.

Unit 13

That is my oldest possession.
Do we need permission to go?

Unit 14

Beth must do some revision.
Dad is building an extension.

Partner 2 dictation sentences

Unit 1

I mistrust that group of girls.

Perhaps you misunderstand me.

Unit 2

That pirate has the treasure.

It was a pleasure to see you.

Unit 3

Grandpa wrote his autobiography.

She used autopilot to land the plane.

Unit 4

The gates opened automatically.

Josh answered the question cheekily.

Unit 5

It was an intercity train.

Mum had an important interview.

Unit 6

They all jumped into the sleigh.

The bird of prey circled the rat.

Unit 7

That film was very humorous.

The lion was courageous.

Unit 8

Cut along the line with the scissors.

Police soon arrived at the scene.

Unit 9

I saw the invasion.

Please describe the collision.

Unit 10

This old letter is illegible.

Remember that stealing is illegal.

Unit 11

That is a grotesque monster.

We are top of the league now.

Unit 12

Sweet apples are irresistible to me.

That is irrelevant to the topic.

Unit 13

I sent my submission for the competition.

My first impression was good.

Unit 14

We could feel the tension before the match.

The questions checked our comprehension.